Meditation Made Easy - A Crash Course for Beginners

Dean Hunter

Published by Dean Hunter, 2023.

MEDITATION MADE EASY - A CRASH COURSE FOR BEGINNERS

First edition. May 10, 2023.

ISBN: 979-8223034193

Written by Dean Hunter.

Table of Contents

DEDICATED TO

Every single reader!

ACKNOWLEDGMENTS
Thanks to you!

The Benefits of Meditation
How It Can Transform Your Life

Meditation is a practice that has been around for thousands of years, and it has been used by people from all walks of life to promote physical, mental, and spiritual well-being. While meditation is often associated with religious and spiritual practices, it has many benefits that go beyond any particular belief system. We will explore the many ways in which meditation can transform your life and bring greater peace, joy, and fulfillment.

Reducing Stress and Anxiety

One of the most well-known benefits of meditation is its ability to reduce stress and anxiety. When we meditate, we are able to quiet the mind and focus on the present moment, which helps to reduce feelings of worry, fear, and overwhelm. Regular meditation practice has been shown to lower levels of the stress hormone cortisol, which can have a positive impact on our physical and emotional health.

Improving Focus and Concentration

Another benefit of meditation is its ability to improve focus and concentration. By practicing mindfulness meditation, we can train our minds to become more aware of our thoughts and feelings, which can help us to better manage distractions and stay focused on the task at hand. Studies have shown that regular meditation practice can increase the density of gray matter in the brain, which is associated with improved memory, attention, and decision-making skills.

Enhancing Emotional Well-being

Meditation can also be a powerful tool for enhancing emotional well-being. When we meditate, we are able to observe our thoughts and feelings without judgment, which can help us to develop greater self-awareness and self-acceptance. This can lead to a greater sense of inner peace and happiness, as well as improved relationships with others.

Improving Sleep

Many people struggle with sleep issues, whether it be difficulty falling asleep or staying asleep throughout the night. Regular meditation practice has been shown to improve sleep quality, reduce insomnia symptoms, and increase feelings of relaxation and well-being. By practicing meditation before bedtime, we can calm our minds and bodies, which can help us to drift off to sleep more easily and stay asleep longer.

Strengthening the Immune System

Meditation can also have a positive impact on our physical health. Studies have shown that regular meditation practice can strengthen the immune system, lower blood pressure, and reduce the risk of chronic diseases such as heart disease and diabetes. By reducing stress and promoting relaxation, meditation can help to support overall health and well-being.

In summary, meditation has many benefits that can positively impact all areas of our lives. From reducing stress and anxiety to improving focus, enhancing emotional well-being, improving sleep, and strengthening the immune system, there are countless reasons why meditation is a valuable tool for promoting health and happiness. By incorporating meditation into our daily routine, we can transform our lives and experience greater peace, joy, and fulfillment.

Setting Yourself Up for Success
Creating a Meditation Practice Space

When it comes to meditation, creating a designated space for your practice can make all the difference in the world. Having a space that is specifically dedicated to meditation can help you get into the right frame of mind and set the tone for your practice. In this chapter, we'll explore how to create the perfect meditation practice space for yourself.

Choose a Quiet Space

The first step in creating a meditation practice space is to choose a quiet and peaceful location. You want to find a space where you can sit and meditate without being disturbed by outside noises or distractions. If possible, choose a room with natural light and ventilation, or add some soft lighting or calming aromas to create a serene atmosphere.

Clear the Space

Once you have found a suitable location, it's time to clear the space. Remove any clutter, distractions or unnecessary items from the area. This will help create a sense of calm and promote a distraction-free environment for your meditation practice. You can even add some decor to make the space feel more personal and inviting.

Choose Your Seating

Next, choose the seating that works best for you. You can opt for a meditation cushion, a yoga mat, or a comfortable chair. Whatever you choose, make sure that it is comfortable and promotes good posture. It's important to note that meditation is not about sitting in a specific way or for a specific amount of time. It's about being comfortable and present in the moment.

Add Some Natural Elements

Integrating natural elements into your meditation practice space can also be helpful. For instance, you can add some plants or flowers, a small water feature or a natural rock. These elements can add a sense of calm and serenity to your meditation practice space.

Include Some Tools

You may also want to include some meditation tools, such as candles, incense, or a bell. These items can help you get into the right mindset and create a sense of ritual and structure to your meditation practice.

Create a Routine

Finally, creating a routine can help you make the most out of your meditation practice space. Try to meditate at the same time every day, even if it's only for a few minutes. This will help you get into the habit of meditating regularly and make it easier to incorporate into your daily life.

Creating a meditation practice space doesn't have to be complicated or expensive. With just a few simple steps, you can create a space that is peaceful, calming, and conducive to your meditation practice. Remember, meditation is a personal journey, so create a space that resonates with you and feels like home.

Posture and Breath
The Foundation of Meditation

When it comes to meditation, posture and breath are the foundation upon which everything else rests. Without proper posture and breath, your meditation practice may be less effective and less comfortable.

Posture is important because it helps you maintain focus and keeps your body comfortable. When you sit with a straight back and an open chest, you allow your lungs to expand fully, making it easier to breathe deeply. This deep breathing helps you to relax and be present in the moment.

Here are some tips for finding the right posture for meditation:

- Sit on a cushion or mat: Sitting on a cushion or mat helps elevate your hips and allows your spine to naturally curve. This takes pressure off your lower back and allows you to sit for longer periods of time.
- Cross your legs: Cross your legs in a way that is comfortable for you. You can sit in a full lotus, half lotus, or even with your legs extended in front of you. The important thing is to find a position that allows you to sit comfortably for an extended period of time.
- Straighten your back: Sit with a straight back, as if there was a string pulling the top of your head toward the ceiling. This helps you to maintain focus and keeps your lungs open and free.
- Relax your shoulders: Allow your shoulders to drop and relax away from your ears. This will help you to sit more comfortably and breathe more easily.

Breathing is the second important aspect of meditation. When you breathe deeply and slowly, you calm your mind and body. This helps you to focus on the present moment and reduces stress and anxiety.

Here are some tips for breathing during meditation:

- Breathe through your nose: Breathing through your nose warms and filters the air, making it easier on your lungs.
- Breathe deeply: Inhale slowly and deeply, filling your lungs with

air. Exhale slowly and completely, allowing your body to release any tension or stress.

- Focus on your breath: As you breathe, focus your attention on the sensation of air moving in and out of your body. This helps you to stay present and focused during your meditation practice.

Remember, meditation is a practice, and it takes time to develop proper posture and breathing techniques. With patience and practice, you can create a strong foundation for your meditation practice that will help you to find peace, clarity, and focus in your daily life.

The Different Types of Meditation Finding What Works for You

Meditation is not a one-size-fits-all practice. There are many different types of meditation, and what works for one person may not work for another. The good news is that with so many options, there is a type of meditation that can suit anyone's personality, preferences, and goals. Here are some of the most popular types of meditation:

- Mindfulness Meditation: This type of meditation is all about being present in the moment and focusing on the sensations in your body, your breath, and your surroundings. It can help you become more aware of your thoughts and emotions and learn how to observe them without judgment.
- Mantra Meditation: Mantra meditation involves repeating a word or phrase, known as a mantra, to help focus the mind and prevent distractions. The word or phrase can be anything, as long as it has meaning to you and is repeated consistently.
- Visualization Meditation: This type of meditation involves creating mental images in your mind, such as visualizing a peaceful scene or imagining yourself accomplishing a goal. It can be a powerful way to tap into your imagination and tap into your subconscious mind.
- Movement Meditation: This type of meditation is all about incorporating physical movement into your practice. Examples include yoga, tai chi, and walking meditation. It can help improve flexibility, balance, and physical awareness while also calming the mind.
- Loving-Kindness Meditation: This type of meditation is focused on cultivating feelings of love, kindness, and compassion towards yourself and others. It involves sending positive thoughts and energy to yourself and others, and can help improve your relationships and overall well-being.
- Transcendental Meditation: This type of meditation involves repeating a specific sound or mantra to help the mind settle into a deep state of relaxation. It is often practiced twice a day for

20 minutes and has been shown to reduce stress and improve overall well-being.

- Body Scan Meditation: This type of meditation involves systematically scanning your body from head to toe, focusing on each part and releasing tension as you go. It can help improve physical awareness and reduce physical discomfort.

It's important to remember that there is no "right" or "wrong" type of meditation. It's all about finding what works for you and your unique needs and preferences. Experiment with different types of meditation to see which ones resonate with you and bring you the most benefits. You can also combine different types of meditation or create your own personalized practice to suit your needs. The most important thing is to make meditation a regular part of your routine and enjoy the journey of self-discovery and inner peace.

Guided Meditation
Using Audio to Enhance Your Practice

What is Guided Meditation?

Guided meditation is a type of meditation where you listen to someone who leads you through a meditation practice, step by step. This person may use a script, music, or other sound effects to create an immersive and relaxing experience. Guided meditations can vary in length, from a few minutes to an hour or more, and can focus on a range of themes, such as relaxation, stress relief, self-love, or inner peace.

Benefits of Guided Meditation

Guided meditation can be an excellent tool for beginners who may struggle with getting started with meditation. It can help you to relax, focus your attention, and be more present in the moment. Other benefits of guided meditation include:

- Increased relaxation: Guided meditation can help you to relax and reduce stress, which can lead to a calmer mind and better sleep.

- Improved focus: The guidance provided in guided meditation can help you to focus your attention, which can improve your concentration and productivity.

- Heightened self-awareness: Guided meditation can help you to become more self-aware by encouraging you to pay attention to your thoughts, emotions, and physical sensations.

- Greater sense of inner peace: Guided meditation can help you to cultivate a sense of inner peace by helping you to let go of stress and negative emotions.

Using Guided Meditation to Enhance Your Practice

If you're new to meditation, guided meditation can be an excellent way to get started. Here are some tips to help you use guided meditation to enhance your practice:

- Find a quiet space: Find a quiet space where you won't be

disturbed, and where you feel comfortable and relaxed.

- Choose a guided meditation that resonates with you: There are many guided meditations available online, so take some time to find one that resonates with you. Look for a meditation that aligns with your goals and intentions.
- Use headphones: Using headphones can help to immerse you in the guided meditation experience and block out any external distractions.
- Practice regularly: Consistency is key when it comes to meditation, so try to practice guided meditation regularly, ideally daily, to experience the benefits fully.
- Experiment with different guided meditations: There are many different types of guided meditations available, so don't be afraid to experiment and try different ones to find what works best for you.

Guided meditation can be a powerful tool for enhancing your meditation practice. It can help you to relax, focus your attention, and cultivate a sense of inner peace. By finding a guided meditation that resonates with you and practicing regularly, you can experience the many benefits of this form of meditation.

Mindfulness Meditation
Cultivating Awareness in the Present Moment

Mindfulness meditation is one of the most popular and effective types of meditation. It involves bringing your attention to the present moment, without judgment or distraction, and learning to observe your thoughts, feelings, and surroundings with openness and curiosity.

This type of meditation has gained popularity in recent years due to its ability to reduce stress, improve emotional regulation, and enhance overall well-being. By developing a non-judgmental awareness of the present moment, mindfulness meditation can help you let go of negative thoughts and emotions, and cultivate a greater sense of calm and clarity.

To begin practicing mindfulness meditation, find a quiet space where you can sit comfortably, without distractions. You may choose to sit on a cushion or chair, with your back straight and your feet flat on the ground. Take a few deep breaths, and then bring your attention to your breath, noticing the sensation of air flowing in and out of your nostrils.

As you focus on your breath, you may notice that your mind begins to wander, perhaps to a thought or feeling that pulls your attention away from the present moment. When this happens, simply notice the thought or feeling, without judging it or getting caught up in it. Then, gently bring your attention back to your breath.

The goal of mindfulness meditation is not to stop your thoughts, but to become more aware of them and how they affect you. Over time, you may begin to notice patterns in your thoughts and emotions, and develop a greater understanding of how they impact your mood and behavior.

One useful technique for practicing mindfulness is the body scan. This involves bringing your attention to different parts of your body, and noticing any sensations or tension you may be holding. Begin at the top of your head, and slowly scan down your body, paying attention to your neck, shoulders, arms, hands, chest, stomach, hips, legs, and feet. If you notice any tension or discomfort, simply observe it, without trying to change it, and then bring your attention back to your breath.

Another technique is to practice mindfulness in daily life, by bringing your attention to your senses and surroundings. For example, when you are eating a meal, take a moment to notice the colors, textures, and flavors of the food. When you are walking, pay attention to the sensation of your feet on the ground, the sounds around you, and the movement of your body.

By practicing mindfulness meditation regularly, you can develop greater self-awareness, reduce stress and anxiety, and improve your overall well-being. It may take time and patience to fully develop this practice, but the benefits are well worth the effort. Remember to approach your practice with curiosity and openness, and to be gentle with yourself as you learn to cultivate a greater sense of mindfulness in your daily life.

Mantra Meditation
Using Sound to Focus Your Mind

What is Mantra Meditation?

Mantra meditation is a form of meditation that uses repetitive sounds, words, or phrases as a tool to focus and calm the mind. The word "mantra" is derived from two Sanskrit words: "manas" meaning mind and "tra" meaning tool or instrument. Mantras are typically chanted or repeated silently during meditation as a way to quiet the mind and access deeper states of consciousness.

Mantras can be a single word, such as "Om," or a phrase, such as "I am peaceful and calm." They can be in any language and can have different meanings, depending on the intention of the practitioner.

Benefits of Mantra Meditation

- Focus: Mantras provide a focal point for the mind, allowing you to stay present and centered in the moment.
- Calm: Repeating a mantra can be soothing and calming, reducing stress and anxiety.
- Clarity: Mantra meditation can help clear the mind and improve mental clarity, allowing you to see things more clearly.
- Spiritual Growth: Mantras can have a spiritual significance and can be used to connect with higher states of consciousness.

How to Practice Mantra Meditation

- Choose a Mantra: Choose a word or phrase that resonates with you and has personal meaning. This can be a traditional mantra, such as "Om," or a phrase that reflects your personal intention, such as "I am at peace."
- Find a Comfortable Seat: Sit in a comfortable cross-legged position, with your spine straight and your hands resting on your knees.
- Focus on the Mantra: Begin to repeat your mantra silently to yourself, allowing your mind to focus solely on the sound and vibration of the mantra. If your mind wanders, gently bring it

back to the mantra.

- Let Go: Allow yourself to let go of any thoughts or distractions, surrendering to the repetition of the mantra.
- Practice Regularly: Practice mantra meditation for at least 10-20 minutes a day, ideally in the same place and at the same time each day.

Tips for Mantra Meditation

- Experiment with different mantras until you find one that resonates with you.
- Try chanting your mantra out loud to feel the vibration of the sound.
- Use a mala or string of beads to keep track of your repetitions.
- If you become distracted, gently bring your mind back to the mantra without judgement.
- Avoid forcing the mantra. Allow it to flow naturally and effortlessly.

Mantra meditation is a powerful tool for calming the mind, improving focus, and connecting with higher states of consciousness. With regular practice and patience, you can experience the many benefits of this ancient practice.

Visualization Meditation
Harnessing the Power of Your Imagination

Visualization meditation, also known as creative visualization, is a type of meditation that involves using your imagination to create vivid mental images.

The Benefits of Visualization Meditation

Visualization meditation has been shown to have numerous benefits, including:

- Reducing stress and anxiety: Visualization meditation can help calm your mind and reduce stress levels. By focusing on positive mental images, you can shift your attention away from worries and concerns, and promote a sense of calm and relaxation.
- Boosting creativity: Visualization meditation can help enhance your creativity by allowing you to explore new ideas and perspectives. By using your imagination, you can access new ways of thinking and problem-solving.
- Improving performance: Visualization meditation can be a powerful tool for improving performance in a variety of areas, such as sports, academics, and public speaking. By visualizing success, you can increase your confidence and motivation.
- Enhancing overall well-being: Visualization meditation can help promote a positive mindset, boost self-esteem, and improve your overall sense of well-being.

Getting Started with Visualization Meditation

To get started with visualization meditation, find a quiet and comfortable place where you can sit or lie down without being disturbed. It can be helpful to create a peaceful environment by lighting candles or playing soothing music.

- Begin by taking a few deep breaths and focusing your attention on your breath. Feel the air moving in and out of your body, and allow yourself to relax.
- Once you feel relaxed, begin to visualize a peaceful scene in your

mind. This could be a beach, a forest, a mountain, or any other place that makes you feel calm and relaxed.

- Use all of your senses to make the scene as vivid as possible. See the colors, hear the sounds, smell the scents, feel the textures, and taste the flavors.

- Spend some time exploring the scene, noticing the details and allowing yourself to fully immerse in the experience.

- If your mind begins to wander, gently bring your attention back to the scene and continue to focus on your breath.

- When you are ready to end your meditation, take a few deep breaths and slowly bring your awareness back to the present moment.

Tips for Deepening Your Practice

Here are some tips to help you deepen your visualization meditation practice:

- Practice regularly: Like any other form of meditation, consistency is key. Aim to practice visualization meditation for at least 10-15 minutes each day.

- Use affirmations: Affirmations are positive statements that can help reprogram your subconscious mind. Incorporate affirmations into your visualization practice to reinforce positive beliefs about yourself and your abilities.

- Be patient: Visualization meditation is a skill that takes time to develop. Be patient with yourself and allow yourself to gradually improve over time.

- Use guided meditations: Guided meditations can be a helpful tool for beginners who are just getting started with visualization meditation. Look for guided meditations online or in books to help guide your practice.

Visualization meditation can be a powerful tool for reducing stress, boosting creativity, and enhancing your overall sense of well-being. By using your imagination to create positive mental images, you can cultivate a more positive mindset and improve your overall quality of life. With regular practice and patience, you can learn to harness the power of your imagination and create the life you desire.

Walking Meditation
Finding Peace in Movement

Meditation doesn't always have to be done in a still, seated position. In fact, walking meditation can be a powerful practice for those who struggle to stay still or find it difficult to sit for extended periods of time. Walking meditation combines the physical act of walking with the mental focus of meditation, making it a great option for those who want to incorporate mindfulness into their daily movement.

Walking meditation offers many of the same benefits as seated meditation, such as reducing stress, improving concentration, and promoting a sense of calm and inner peace. However, it also offers some unique benefits that make it a worthwhile practice to explore.

For one, walking meditation can be a great way to get some exercise while still practicing mindfulness. By combining the physical movement of walking with the mental focus of meditation, you can create a more holistic approach to your health and wellbeing.

Additionally, walking meditation can be a great way to connect with nature and the world around you. As you walk, you can take in the sights, sounds, and smells of your surroundings, allowing you to be fully present in the moment and appreciate the beauty of the world around you.

How to Practice Walking Meditation

- Find a quiet, safe space where you can walk without distractions. This could be a park, a quiet street, or even just a long hallway in your home.
- Stand still for a moment and take a few deep breaths, allowing yourself to settle into the present moment.
- Begin walking at a slow, steady pace, paying close attention to the physical sensations of your body as you move. Notice the feeling of your feet touching the ground, the movement of your legs, and the way your arms swing naturally at your sides.
- As you walk, focus your attention on your breath. You might count your breaths, or simply notice the way the air feels moving in and out of your body.
- If your mind starts to wander, gently bring your attention back

to your breath and the physical sensations of your body.

- As you continue to walk, try to maintain this focus on your breath and the present moment. You can also try to expand your awareness to include the world around you, taking in the sights, sounds, and sensations of your surroundings.
- When you're ready to finish your practice, gradually slow your pace and come to a stop. Take a few moments to notice how you feel, and take a few deep breaths before returning to your day.

Tips for Practicing Walking Meditation

- Start with short sessions, such as 5-10 minutes, and gradually increase your practice over time.
- Experiment with different walking speeds and environments to find what feels most comfortable for you.
- If you find it difficult to maintain your focus on your breath, you can try silently repeating a mantra or phrase to yourself as you walk.
- Try to walk with a soft gaze, rather than focusing too intently on any one object or point.
- Don't worry too much about "getting it right." Walking meditation is a practice, and like any practice, it takes time and patience to develop.

Overcoming Obstacles
How to Deal with Distractions and Discomfort

Meditation is a practice that requires focus, patience, and dedication. While it can be a transformative experience, it can also be challenging to maintain a consistent practice. Distractions and discomfort are common obstacles that beginners may face. Fortunately, there are strategies and techniques you can use to overcome these obstacles and deepen your practice.

Dealing with Distractions

Distractions are a natural part of the meditation process. Our minds are constantly bombarded with thoughts, emotions, and sensations that can take us away from the present moment. Here are some tips to help you deal with distractions during meditation:

- Acknowledge the distraction: When you become aware of a distraction, simply acknowledge it and gently bring your attention back to your breath or the object of your meditation. Avoid judging yourself or getting frustrated, as this can make it harder to let go of the distraction.
- Use a mantra: A mantra is a word or phrase that you repeat to yourself during meditation. This can help you focus your attention and bring your mind back to the present moment. Examples of mantras include "peace," "calm," or "let go."
- Try guided meditation: Guided meditation is a form of meditation where a teacher or guide walks you through the process. This can be especially helpful for beginners who are easily distracted or have trouble focusing.
- Experiment with different types of meditation: Not all types of meditation are right for everyone. If you find yourself getting distracted during one type of meditation, try another. You may find that a different approach works better for you.

Dealing with Discomfort

Discomfort is another common obstacle that beginners may face during meditation. This can take the form of physical discomfort, such as aches or pains, or emotional discomfort, such as anxiety or restlessness. Here are some strategies for dealing with discomfort during meditation:

- Adjust your posture: If you're experiencing physical discomfort, try adjusting your posture. Sit on a cushion or chair, and make sure your spine is straight and your shoulders are relaxed. This can help alleviate tension in your body and make you more comfortable.
- Practice self-compassion: Be kind to yourself during meditation. If you're experiencing discomfort, acknowledge it and try to be gentle with yourself. Avoid pushing yourself too hard or getting frustrated, as this can make the discomfort worse.
- Focus on your breath: If you're feeling anxious or restless, try focusing on your breath. Take slow, deep breaths and try to match the length of your inhales and exhales. This can help calm your mind and body.
- Use visualization: Visualization is a technique where you imagine yourself in a peaceful, relaxing environment. This can help alleviate emotional discomfort and create a sense of calm. Imagine yourself in a beautiful, natural setting, such as a forest or beach, and focus on the sights, sounds, and sensations around you.

Distractions and discomfort are common obstacles that beginners may face during meditation. However, with practice and patience, you can learn to overcome these obstacles and deepen your practice. By acknowledging distractions and discomfort, adjusting your approach, and practicing self-compassion, you can cultivate a deeper sense of focus and inner peace. Remember that meditation is a journey, and each moment is an opportunity to learn and grow.

Tips for Staying Consistent
Making Meditation a Habit

One of the most challenging aspects of starting a meditation practice is making it a habit. Just like any new behavior, it takes time and effort to establish a regular routine. But with some simple tips and tricks, you can make meditation a consistent part of your daily life.

- Start small: When you're first starting out, don't try to meditate for an hour a day. It's better to start with just a few minutes each day and gradually work your way up. Even just five minutes a day can make a big difference.
- Set a regular time: Try to meditate at the same time every day. This will help you establish a routine and make meditation a habit. Many people find that meditating first thing in the morning or before bed works well for them.
- Create a dedicated space: Designate a space in your home that is just for meditation. It doesn't have to be a big space – just a corner of your bedroom or living room will do. Set up a cushion or chair and any other items that help you feel comfortable and relaxed.
- Use reminders: Set reminders on your phone or calendar to meditate each day. You can also use visual cues, such as leaving your meditation cushion out where you can see it.
- Find an accountability partner: Find a friend or family member who also wants to start a meditation practice. Check in with each other regularly to share your progress and offer support.
- Be kind to yourself: It's normal to miss a day or two of meditation here and there. Don't beat yourself up about it. Just pick up where you left off and keep going.
- Mix it up: Don't be afraid to try different types of meditation or techniques to keep your practice fresh and interesting. You can also attend meditation classes or workshops to learn new skills and connect with other meditators.
- Make it enjoyable: Incorporate things into your meditation

practice that you enjoy, such as burning candles, using essential oils, or listening to calming music. This will help make meditation a relaxing and enjoyable experience.

Remember, the key to making meditation a habit is consistency. By following these tips and making meditation a regular part of your daily routine, you'll soon find that it becomes second nature. And the more you practice, the more you'll experience the many benefits of meditation in your life.

Deepening Your Practice
Advanced Techniques for Experienced Meditators

Congratulations on your journey of meditation so far! You have learned about the different types of meditation, overcome obstacles, and established a consistent practice. Now, you may be wondering how to take your practice to the next level and deepen your experience.

In this chapter, we will explore some advanced techniques for experienced meditators to help you explore deeper levels of awareness and consciousness.

Yoga Nidra, also known as yogic sleep, is a deep relaxation practice that involves lying down and listening to a guided meditation. It is said to be as restful as a full night's sleep, and can help you access deep levels of consciousness. During the practice, you remain in a state between waking and sleeping, allowing your mind to enter a deeply relaxed state. Many people report feeling refreshed and rejuvenated after a yoga nidra session.

Vipassana, which means "insight" or "clear seeing," is a meditation technique that involves observing the breath and bodily sensations. The practice involves sitting in silence for extended periods of time, typically 10 days or longer. During this time, you learn to observe your thoughts and emotions without judgment, allowing you to gain insight into your own mind and behavior. While it can be challenging, many people find Vipassana to be a life-changing experience.

Transcendental Meditation (TM) is a popular form of meditation that involves the use of a mantra, or sound, to focus the mind. The technique is said to promote relaxation, reduce stress, and increase self-awareness. During the practice, you sit comfortably with your eyes closed and silently repeat a mantra to yourself. The practice is typically taught by a certified TM teacher and requires a financial investment.

Loving-kindness meditation, also known as metta meditation, is a practice that involves generating feelings of love and compassion towards yourself and others. The practice involves silently repeating phrases of well-wishes and goodwill towards yourself, loved ones, acquaintances, and even those who may have hurt you in the past. Many people find that this practice helps cultivate a greater sense of empathy and kindness towards themselves and others.

Chakra meditation involves focusing on the energy centers, or chakras, in the body. The practice involves visualizing each chakra and the color associated with it, as well as repeating mantras associated with each chakra. The goal is to balance and activate each chakra, promoting physical, emotional, and spiritual wellbeing.

Sound meditation involves listening to different types of sound, such as singing bowls or gongs, to promote relaxation and mindfulness. The practice involves lying down or sitting comfortably and allowing the sound vibrations to wash over you, promoting a deep sense of relaxation and inner peace.

There are many advanced techniques that experienced meditators can explore to deepen their practice. Whether you choose to try yoga nidra, Vipassana, TM, loving-kindness meditation, chakra meditation, or sound meditation, remember that the goal of meditation is not to achieve a certain state or experience, but to simply be present and cultivate awareness. Experiment with different techniques and find what works best for you, and always approach your practice with curiosity, openness, and compassion.

Meditation and the Mind-Body Connection
How It Impacts Your Physical Health

Meditation has been shown to have numerous benefits for both the mind and body. In this chapter, we will explore the ways in which meditation impacts your physical health and well-being.

The mind-body connection is a powerful one. Our thoughts, emotions, and physical sensations are all interconnected. When we are stressed or anxious, our body responds with physical symptoms such as a faster heart rate, shallow breathing, and tense muscles. Conversely, when we are calm and relaxed, our body responds with physical sensations such as slower breathing, a slower heart rate, and relaxed muscles.

Meditation helps to cultivate a state of relaxation and calmness, which has a positive impact on our physical health. Here are some of the ways in which meditation can improve our physical well-being:

- Reduces stress: Stress has a negative impact on our physical health, leading to conditions such as high blood pressure, heart disease, and stroke. Meditation has been shown to reduce stress levels by lowering cortisol, the stress hormone, in the body.

- Improves immune function: Research has found that regular meditation practice can boost the immune system, making us more resistant to illness and disease.

- Lowers blood pressure: High blood pressure is a risk factor for heart disease and stroke. Meditation has been shown to lower blood pressure, reducing the risk of these conditions.

- Eases pain: Chronic pain can have a significant impact on our physical and mental well-being. Meditation has been shown to reduce pain levels and improve our ability to cope with pain.

- Improves sleep: Poor sleep has been linked to a range of physical health problems, including obesity, diabetes, and heart disease. Meditation can help to improve sleep quality and duration, leading to better overall health.

- Reduces inflammation: Chronic inflammation is linked to a range of health conditions, including arthritis, asthma, and heart disease. Meditation has been shown to reduce inflammation in the body, improving overall health.

- Enhances athletic performance: Meditation can improve focus, concentration, and mental clarity, all of which can enhance athletic performance.

In addition to these physical benefits, meditation can also have a positive impact on our mental and emotional well-being. By reducing stress, anxiety, and depression, meditation can improve our overall quality of life.

It's important to note that while meditation can have significant benefits for our physical health, it should not be used as a substitute for medical treatment. If you have any medical conditions, it's important to consult with your healthcare provider before starting a meditation practice.

The mind-body connection is a powerful one, and meditation can have a significant impact on our physical health and well-being. By reducing stress, improving immune function, lowering blood pressure, easing pain, improving sleep, reducing inflammation, and enhancing athletic performance, meditation can help us to lead healthier, happier lives.

Conclusion
Embracing the Journey of Meditation

Congratulations on completing this crash course on meditation! By now, you have gained a deeper understanding of what meditation is, how it can benefit your life, and how to establish a regular practice.

Meditation is not a one-time activity, but a lifelong journey of self-discovery, growth, and transformation. As you continue to meditate, you will discover new depths within yourself, gain greater clarity of mind, and cultivate inner peace and joy.

Remember, meditation is not a quick fix, but a gradual process of cultivating new habits, transforming your mind and body, and integrating mindfulness into your daily life. It takes time, patience, and dedication to see the long-term benefits.

Here are a few key takeaways to help you embrace the journey of meditation:

- Consistency is key: Try to meditate daily, even if it's just for a few minutes. This will help you build momentum and establish a regular practice.
- Experiment with different techniques: There are many types of meditation, so try a variety of techniques to find what works best for you. Don't be afraid to mix and match different techniques.
- Be kind to yourself: Meditation is not about perfection or achieving a certain outcome. It's about being present and kind to yourself, no matter what thoughts or emotions arise during your practice.
- Cultivate mindfulness in your daily life: Meditation is not just a practice you do on the cushion, but a way of living your life with greater awareness and presence. Bring mindfulness to your daily activities, such as eating, walking, or interacting with others.
- 5. Seek support: If you're struggling with your practice, don't hesitate to seek support from a teacher or a meditation group. They can offer guidance, motivation, and inspiration along the

way.

Remember, meditation is a journey, not a destination. Embrace the ups and downs of the journey, and trust that the practice will continue to unfold and enrich your life in unexpected ways. May your journey be filled with peace, joy, and inner wisdom.

ABOUT THE AUTHOR
Simply happy.